Dirt Simple Mountain Dulcimer

by Madeline MacNeil   DISCARD

 www.melbay.com/30362BCDEB

Audio Contents

1	DAA Tuning	11	Red River Valley
2	Are You Sleeping?	12	Be Thou My Vision
3	Skip To My Lou	13	Waterbound
4	Amazing Grace	14	DAD Tuning
5	Swing Low, Sweet Chariot	15	Down In The Valley
6	Auld Lang Syne	16	Boil That Cabbage Down
7	Cockles and Mussels	17	Old Joe Clark
8	Aura Lee	18	Brahms' Lullaby
9	Simple Gifts	19	Mississippi Sawyer
10	Long, Long Ago	20	Twinkle, Twinkle Little Star

Visit us on the Web at www.melbay.com — E-mail us at email@melbay.com

Introduction

You've chosen a very special instrument to play and I look forward to working with you. The mountain dulcimer has a long and interesting history, with much of it being with the residents of Virginia's Shenandoah Valley, West Virginia, western North Carolina and eastern Kentucky. Because of the oral tradition of songs and stories in these areas, the instrument adapted and grew to become what we play today.

We will explore your dulcimer to learn skills like tuning, strumming, finding notes and string changing. You'll know most of the songs in this book while others are possibly unfamiliar. I did this on purpose. How do you take your instrument from the first step and help it grow from there? How do you take a tune, familiar or not, and help it become part of your dulcimer? We have an adventure to explore together!

It is important for you to play music and enjoy your dulcimer. I am here with you as so many people have been with me during my dulcimer journey. Many thanks go to John Burns, Will Shenk, Sue and Michael Ford, Rick Hopper, Betty Berry, Dorothy Lowe, Ellen Morgan, Renee Lavitz, and my dulcimer students throughout the years who have taught me so much. Thank you!

In harmony,
Maddie MacNeil

Contents

Dulcimer Fretboard

Look at the two diagrams that follow. Which one looks like the fret pattern on your dulcimer? What are frets? They're the metal bars stretching across the playing surface (we call it a fretboard) of the instrument. The frets are numbered so when we play music using tablature (more about that soon), we know where to put our fingers.

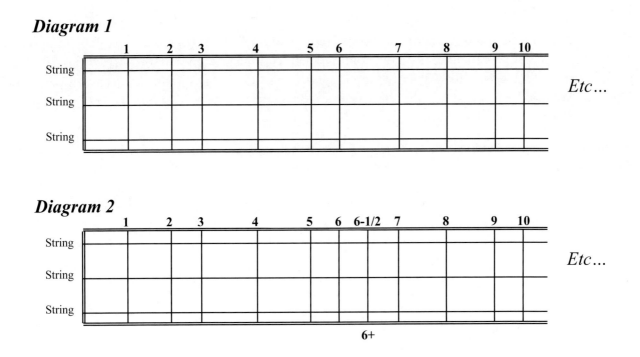

Which looks like the fret pattern on your dulcimer? It's always possible that you have an instrument with additional frets, but most dulcimers are like diagram 1 or 2. The difference is in the middle area of the fretboard. Diagram 2 has an extra fret which we call 6-1/2. In the written music we indicate this as 6+ since it's easier to read 6+ faster than 6-1/2.

When these diagrams are repeated throughout the book, I'll use Diagram 2. (If yours is like Diagram 1, just ignore the extra 6+ fret.) Most dulcimers built today have the extra fret. Yours most likely does. As long as dulcimers have been built, people have adapted them for the notes they wanted for beloved tunes and songs. Around 1960, the standard dulcimers began their journey of including the 6+ fret because of different tunings enjoyed by the players. The reason it's called 6+ is because it is an extra fret to the "standard" instrument.

Dead Fret

Look at the left area of your dulcimer—the area by the tuning pegs. Does your instrument have a fret very close to what we call the nut, where you cannot place your finger to play a note?

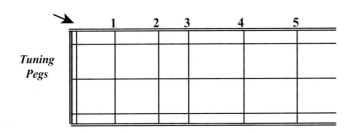

This is called a dead fret. Builders sometimes use them to help with the sound or pitches of the instrument. It's a dead fret because we don't include it in our fret counts.

Tuning The Dulcimer

Because of the musical layout of the dulcimer's fretboard we need to understand tunings. Most of us use one tuning most or all of the time and do just fine. In this book we'll mainly use DAA and, later, DAD. These are the most common tunings used by dulcimer players. Eventually you'll decide which (DAA, DAD or something else) is the best tuning for you, but if you practice with your tuning and feel comfortable, you can re-tune whenever and however you wish. I encourage that!

It's time to go shopping for a tuner. There are various types and brands. Perhaps one's available on your iPhone or other mobile device. A visit to dulcimer stores online or a local music shop will also help. If you go to a music shop local to you, tell the good folks there that the range of your dulcimer is generally from D below Middle C to the D just above Middle C. Trust me; they'll have ones that are fine for the pitches you need and extend higher and lower for other instruments such as the guitar.

Let's assume you now have a tuner. The electronic tuners can hear where you are and, when you pluck a string, it will indicate whether the pitch you have is lower, higher or right on.

Here are the dulcimer strings and their pitches for a DAA tuning—the tuning we'll first use.

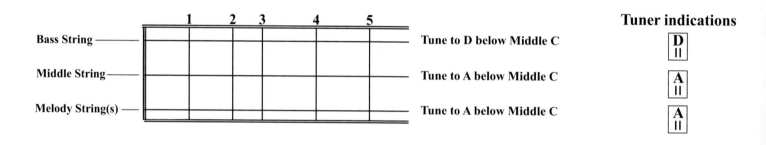

Always be cautious! Strings can break—and they will if they're very old or you tune them higher than they should be. Now set the dulcimer on your lap (tuning pegs to your left) or on a table (pegs to your left).

I like to tune beginning with the bass string on the dulcimer, then the middle string followed by the melody string(s). Starting with the bass string, pluck the string and see if the tuner says the pitch is higher or lower than D. If you need to change the pitch (most likely, if your instrument hasn't been tuned in a while), pluck the string with your right hand and turn the tuning peg gently until you determine which direction moves the pitch in the direction you want. Be gentle. I could use the word "gentle" in practically every sentence about tuning, but as long as you tune gently, I won't repeat the word again—or often.

If the tuner indicates that the pitch of the bass string is another note rather than D, this is where your knowledge of the alphabet is important! Suppose the tuner says C♯ and it looks something like this: C♯

You're not far from D, so tune the string up (in this case) using the following procedure:

Pluck the string • Turn the peg a little • Pluck the string • Turn the peg a little

Continue doing this until the tuner indicates you have reached D. D

If there is a significant difference between the D we want for the bass string—C or E, for example—you may need the help of someone who often tunes instruments, such as guitars. Later in this book we'll discuss string changing, but here's a way to learn more about the tuning capabilities of the strings you now have.

Push and/or pull on a string gently. (There's that word again!) If the string is flexible, you're pretty safe tuning it higher. If it is very taut, don't go higher as it's not far from snapping. This may be the time to refer to the string changing section.

After you've tuned the bass string to D below Middle C, tune the middle string to A below Middle C.

Now to the melody string. You may have one melody string…

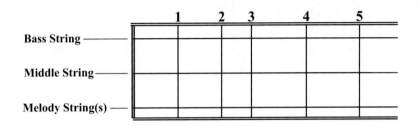

…or two melody strings,

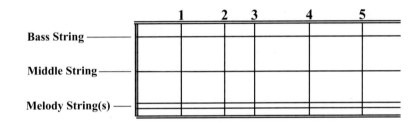

and whichever you have is fine. In any diagrams to follow I'll have one string instead of two. When you have two melody strings they'll be tuned to the same note.

Tune your melody string(s) to A below Middle C.

You are now tuned (from bass to melody string): D A A

Curiosity Corner

Why did you name the strings bass, middle, etc., when on a guitar, for example, they're called E, 1st, or whatever?

Tunings on the dulcimer are changed more often than on a guitar. The terms bass, middle and melody are used by most dulcimer players because, despite the tuning, melodies are usually played on the melody string—the one closest to us. The middle string is obviously in the middle. The bass string has the lowest tone, so the name bass fits.

Holding The Dulcimer

We're getting ready to play a tune. But first, let's put the dulcimer on your lap. Sit on a comfortable chair that has no arms. A bench is also good. Place the dulcimer on your lap, tuning pegs to your left.

Look at the diagrams below. One has the dulcimer straight across the lap. The other has the dulcimer slightly tilted forward.

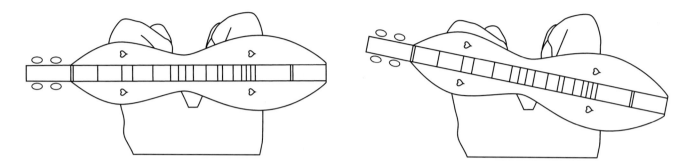

The slight tilt generally makes it easier to play higher tones and to balance the dulcimer on your lap.

Press your left hand on the fretboard near the 2nd or 3rd fret. Does the instrument tilt to your left? It should be steady, so experiment with the location of the dulcimer. I like to suggest that the 3rd fret area be on your left knee.

3rd fret

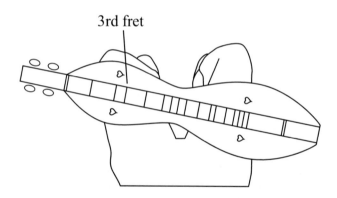

Keeping the dulcimer sturdier on your lap

You can put a bit of wood—or a tiny foot stool—under your left foot; or put a bit of rubbery material, like the items that help you open jars or keep things from slipping on a shelf, on one knee or both knees under the dulcimer. Warning! If you use the rubbery material *do not* leave these pads under or on top of the dulcimer when you're not playing it. They *will* adhere to the instrument fairly soon.

Straps are nice accessories for the dulcimer, especially if your legs are short. A dulcimer shop, or even a local music shop, can help you with the strap. An instrument builder can attach the strap buttons if you prefer.

Dulcimer Picks

Herdim Pick

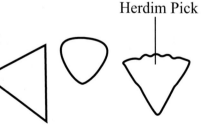

If, say, six of us discuss our favorite tooth brushes, we will probably have six winners. It's the same with picks. There are variations in sizes, weights, lengths, etc. Many dulcimer players enjoy Herdim picks, which are available from dulcimer shops. A visit to a music shop, where you can hold and sample music picks, is a good option.

Strumming

With the dulcimer resting comfortably on your lap, drop your arms on top of the instrument as if you were taking a little rest. Where is your right arm? That is a comfortable area to strum. Now strum across the fretboard, away from you to just beyond the bass string. Let's call that an Out-Strum.

Do that again and compare your strum with the diagrams below.

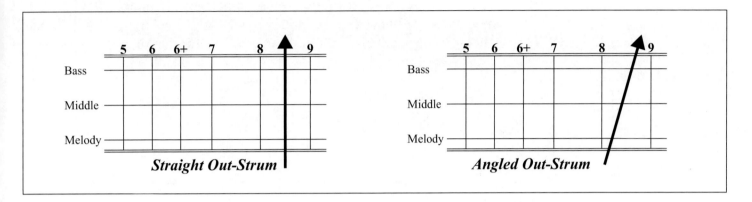

The angled strum is less stressful and less tiring in the long run because your arm is more relaxed. Promise me you'll angle your strum—and begin and end your strums slightly before and after the fretboard, like above.

Playing Notes on the Dulcimer

We're now going to play a song, "Are You Sleeping?" First, we'll discuss where to put your left-hand fingers on the fretboard. We say, or put in the written music, that you put your finger at, for example, the 3rd fret. Which finger and exactly where?

I suggest that you use your index or middle finger—or even both of them together—as a start. They're strong fingers and work well. Eventually you'll decide which fingers work best for you to play tunes comfortably and easily. Our example is the 3rd fret on the melody string. Place your finger just to the left of the 3rd fet, leaving a little space between your finger and the fret.

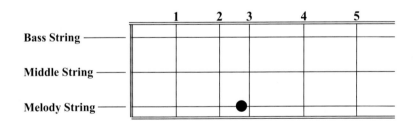

This gives you a clean, pure sound. With your finger at the 3rd fret, melody string (as above), strum all of the strings with an angled Out-Strum. If it sounds clunky, press harder and try again. You could be too close to the metal fret. If so, remember the needed little space. When you get a nice clean sound, play the following notes:

Are	you	sleep - ing?	Are	you	sleep - ing?
3	4	5	3	3	4	5	3

Congratulations! Now let's explore more of the melody notes and the strumming for this song.

Are You Sleeping? • Talked Through

↑ Indicates Out-Strums

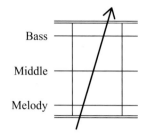

Bass

Middle

Melody

↓ Indicates In-Strums

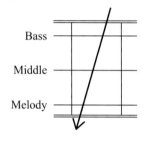

Bass

Middle

Melody

OS
Indicates Out-Strum

IS
Indicates In-Strum

0
Indicates the *open string*. (No left-hand fingers are on the fretboard.)

Are	you	sleep - ing?	Are	you	sleep - ing?
3	**4**	**5** **3**	**3**	**4**	**5** **3**
↑	↑	↑ ↑	↑	↑	↑ ↑

Continuing with the song, do you see where some extra strumming would make the tune more interesting? The fret numbers for Brother John are 5 • 6 • 7, but you're holding the note longer for the word "John." Try the following with Out-Strums and In-Strums.

Bro - ther	John?			Bro - ther	John?		
5 **6**	**7**	**7**	**7**	**5** **6**	**7**	**7**	**7**
↑ ↑	↑	↑	↓	↑ ↑	↑	↑	↓

The most difficult part of this song is the "Morning bells are ringing" part because you're moving more and strumming out and in. Here's a way to practice:

Exercise 1 • Slide your left-hand finger(s) on the melody string to these frets:
7 8 7 6 5 3, 7 8 7 6 5 3

Exercise 2 • With your right hand, strum the open strings (meaning no left-hand fingers are at the frets) and say the words:

Morn - ing	bells	are	ring - ing.	Morn - ing	bells	are	ring - ing.
OS IS	OS	IS	OS OS	OS IS	OS	IS	OS OS

Play Exercises 1 and 2 until they each feel comfortable. Now do Exercises 1 and 2 together—moving your left-hand fingers and doing the In- and Out-strums.

Morn - ing	bells	are	ring - ing.	Morn - ing	bells	are	ring - ing.
7 **8**	**7**	**6**	**5** **3**	**7** **8**	**7**	**6**	**5** **3**
↑ ↓	↑	↓	↑ ↑	↑ ↓	↑	↓	↑ ↑

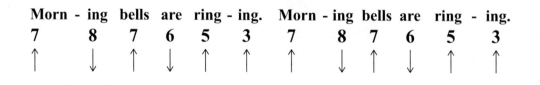

Ding	Dong	Ding.			Ding	Dong	Ding.		
3	**0**	**3**	**3**	**3**	**3**	**0**	**3**	**3**	**3**
↑		↑	↑	↓	↑		↑	↑	↓

The hardest part of this song was "Morning bells are ringing." When you're working on music there's always a more difficult part somewhere. Working through those sections using Exercises 1 and 2 will help you. Now we're going to play "Are You Sleeping?" using tablature, which we'll use in the rest of the book.

Are You Sleeping?
Exploring Tablature

Tune D A A

French Nursery Song
(English Translation)

Before you play this song, I suggest you look at the info at the bottom...

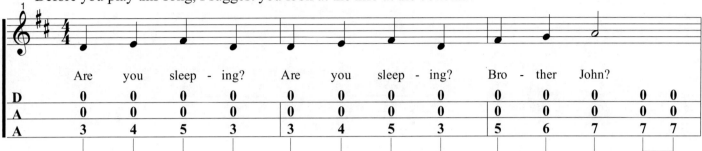

		Are	you	sleep -	ing?	Are	you	sleep -	ing?	Bro -	ther	John?	
D		0	0	0	0	0	0	0	0	0	0	0	0 0
A		0	0	0	0	0	0	0	0	0	0	0	0 0
A		3	4	5	3	3	4	5	3	5	6	7	7 7

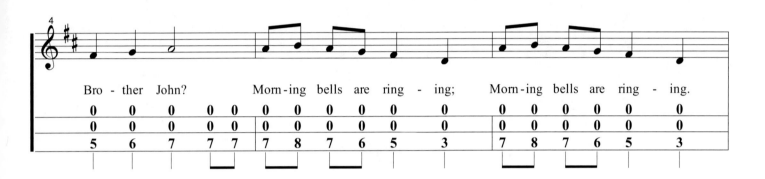

	Bro -	ther	John?		Morn -ing	bells	are	ring	-	ing;	Morn -ing	bells	are	ring	-	ing.
0	0	0	0	0	0	0	0	0	0	0	0	0	0	0	0	0
0	0	0	0	0	0	0	0	0	0	0	0	0	0	0	0	0
	5	6	7	7 7	7	8	7	6	5	3	7	8	7	6	5	3

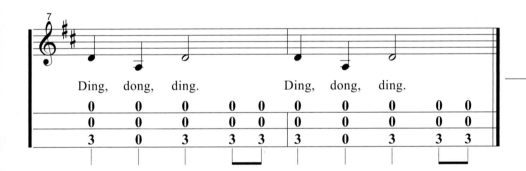

	Ding,	dong,	ding.			Ding,	dong,	ding.	
0	0	0	0	0	0	0	0	0	0
0	0	0	0	0	0	0	0	0	0
3	0	3	3	3	3	0	3	3	3

Tune DAA, at the top left, tells you which tuning to use on the dulcimer for this song.

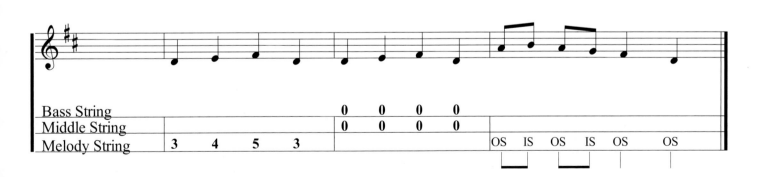

Bass String					0	0	0	0						
Middle String					0	0	0	0						
Melody String	3	4	5	3					OS	IS	OS	IS	OS	OS

Numbers indicate at which fret you put your fingers on the melody string.

The zeros mean you strum these strings open—no fingers at any frets.

Strum Indications
OS = Out-Strum
IS = In-Strum

9

Skip To My Lou
Strumming Choices

Tune D A A

Traditional American Dance Song

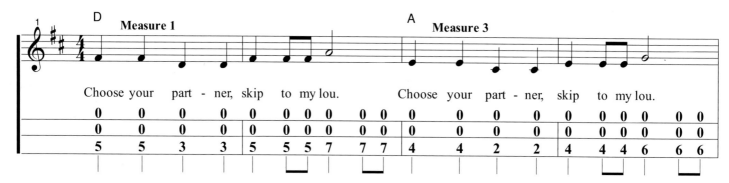

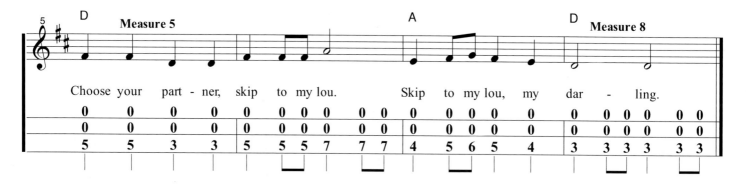

Lost my partner, what'll I do? (3x)
Skip to my lou, my darling.

I'll find another one, prettier, too. (3x)
Skip to my lou, my darling.

Can't get a red bird; blue bird'll do. (3x)
Skip to my lou, my darling.

Flies in the sugarbowl, shoo fly, shoo. (3x)
Skip to my lou, my darling.

The letters over the musical notes…D and A for this song…tell a backup musician (a guitarist, for example) which chords to play.

Choices

We've mentioned your strumming choices before, but here's an example. Look above and below at measures 1, 3 and 5. Below I've added more strums to those measures. When you're playing the song, if you would like to add more strums to any or all of those measures, go for it. Look at measure 8 above and below. If you'd like less strums, especially the last time you play the tune, substitute the strums below. Again, this takes a tune and makes it more your own.

Amazing Grace

Practicing In- and Out-Strums

Tune D A A

Traditional Melody
Lyrics by John Newton (1725-1807)

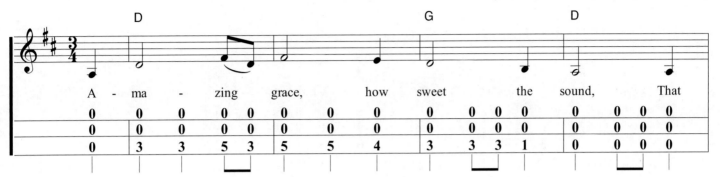

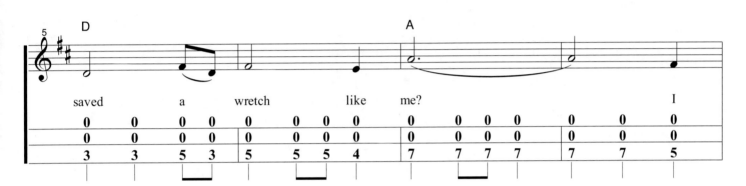

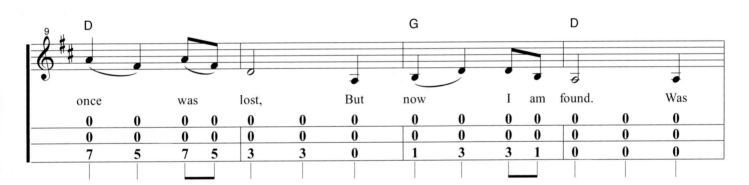

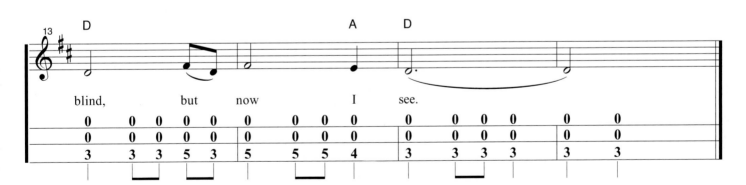

Through many dangers, toils and snares
I have already come.
'Tis grace that brought me safe thus far,
And grace will lead me home.

When we've been there ten thousand years,
Bright shining as the sun,
We've no less days to sing God's praise
Than when we first begun.

Swing Low, Sweet Chariot
Adding Some Chords to our Music
Before playing this song, read the paragraph at the bottom

Tune D A A

American Spiritual

If you look at the chords above the music (D, G and A), I added a tab number on the middle string for the G chord and a tab number on the bass string for the A-chord. Try them! You'll probably find the A chord tab numbers a bit easier at first. What fingers do you use? When I'm playing chords I often use my thumb on the melody string. In measure 2 (chariot) I play that with my thumb at 3 on the melody string, then my little finger on 1 on the melody string. I use my ring finger at 1 on the middle string. In the last measure of the first line, I use my thumb on 7 on the melody string and my index finger on 7 on the bass string. You're *always* welcome to leave out the harmony notes right now and play the melody with open middle and bass strings if you prefer.

Auld Lang Syne
Dotted Quarter Note and Eighth Note Practice

Tune D A A

Scotland

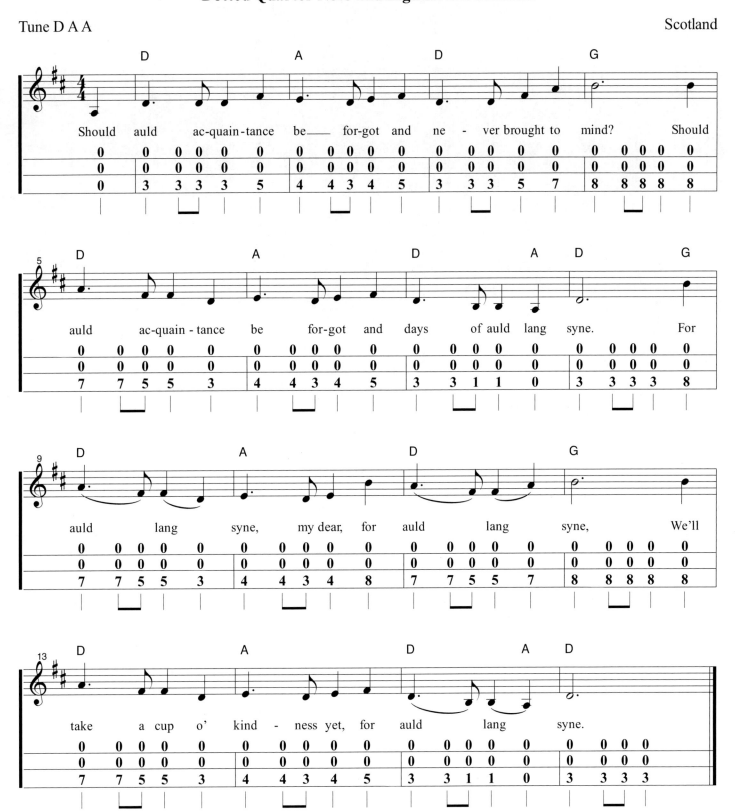

There are many songs and tunes which follow a format we can call "dotted quarter note followed by an eighth note." This song is an example. You'll be changing the fret and the sung word on the In-Strum. Look at the 2nd measure above with the words "be forgot and." You're strumming that measure Out-Strum, Out-Strum, In-Strum, Out-Strum, Out-Strum. The "for-" part of "forgot" is sung and played with an In-Strum.

Even if you don't read music, look at the musical notes. They may help you understand this process.

13

Cockles and Mussels

Strumming Decisions

Tune D A A

Traditional Irish

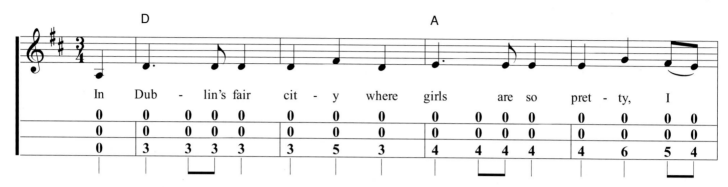

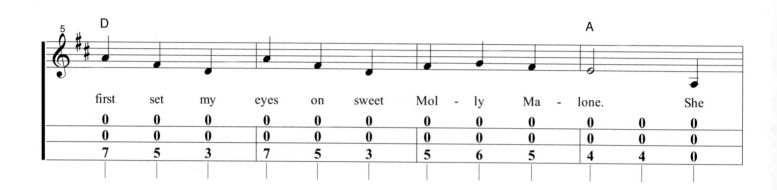

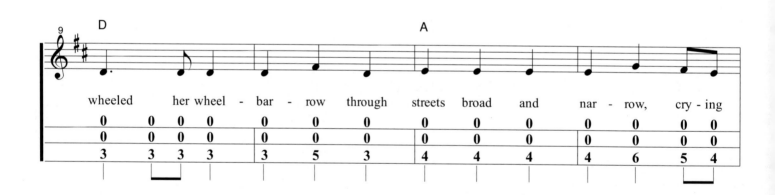

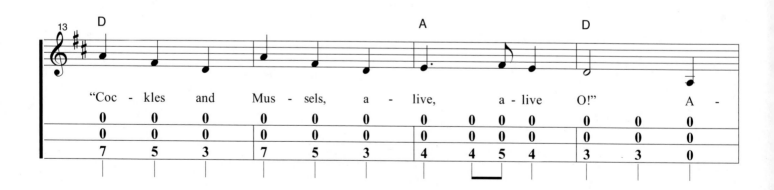

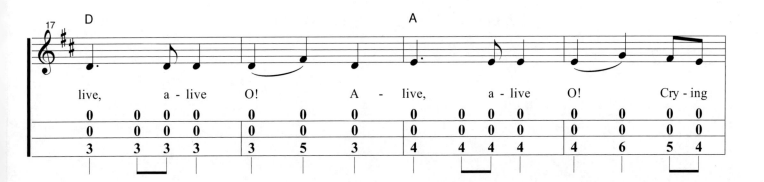

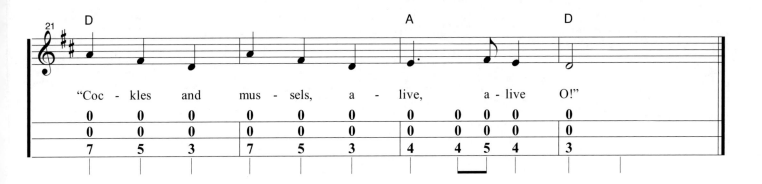

She was a fish monger, and sure 'twas no wonder,
For so were her father and mother before.
They both wheeled their barrows
Through streets broad and narrow,
Crying, "Cockles and mussels, alive, alive O!"
Alive, alive O! Alive, alive O!
Crying "Cockles and mussels, alive, alive O!"

She died of the fever, and no one could save her,
And that was the end of sweet Molly Malone.
But her ghost wheels her barrow
Through streets broad and narrow,
Crying, "Cockles and mussels, alive, alive O!"
Alive, alive O! Alive, alive O!
Crying "Cockles and mussels, alive, alive O!"

This is a time for considering *your own* strumming through a tune or song, especially when notes are being held longer. An example is the last measure of the 2nd line. (If you look at the measure numbers at the beginning of each line, you'll see this is measure 8). For the strums, I have *Out, Out, Out*. Perhaps you like *Out, Out-In, Out* better. Go for it!

Our folk music is arranged in a suggested format, mainly in the rhythmic sense. If I played this song for you five times, without looking at the music, I assure you my Out-Strums and In-Strums would be different more than once in the places where notes are held longer—like measure 8. You put the music inside *you* and play it *your* way.

Aura Lee
A Beautiful Song for your Repertoire

George R. Poulton, Music
W. W. Fosdick, Lyrics
1861

Tune D A A

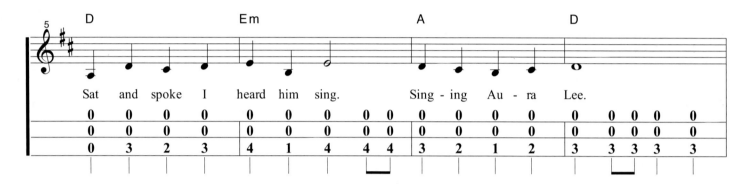

Refrain:

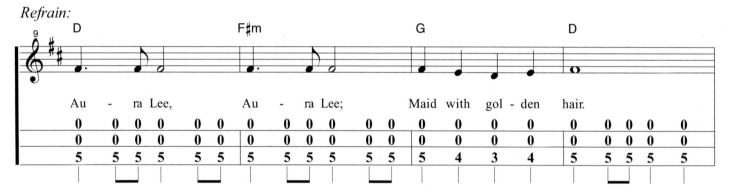

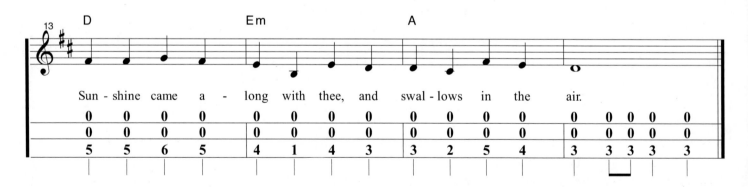

On her cheek the rose was born,	Take my heart, take my ring,	Aura Lee, the birds may flee
Music when she spoke.	I give my all to thee.	The willow's golden hair.
In her eyes the light of morn,	Take me for eternity,	Then the wint'ry wind may be,
With glorious splendor broke.	Dearest Aura Lee.	Blowing everywhere.
Refrain... (Measure 9 to the end)	*Refrain... (Measure 9 to the end)*	*Refrain... (Measure 9 to the end)*

Simple Gifts

Strumming and Moving Left-Hand Fingers

Tune D A A   Shaker Song

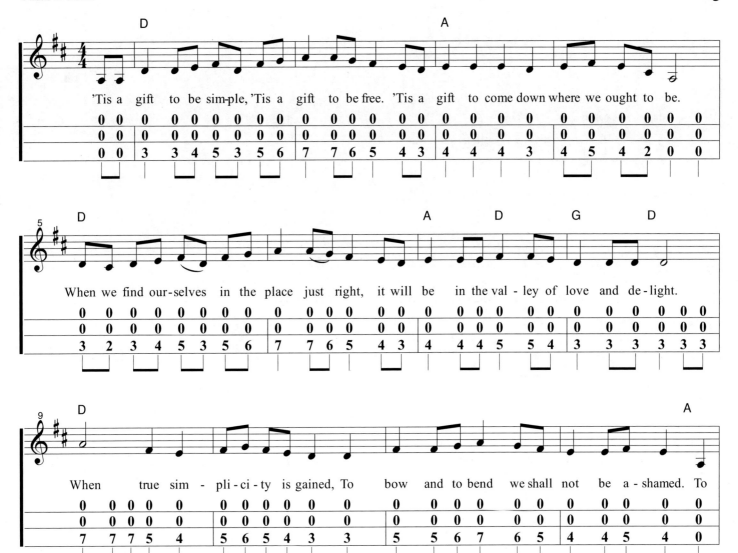

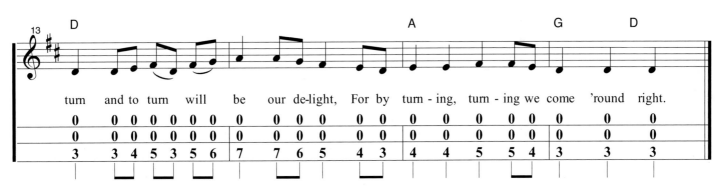

This beautiful Shaker song is a wonderful practice for strumming and moving left-hand fingers. Remember when you were asked to practice the 'Morning Bells Are Ringing' part of "Are You Sleeping" with the right-hand strumming and then with the left-hand note moving? Try that with this song. It is always helpful if you say the words—or even "Da da da da..." when you're practicing the parts. One nice reward when you're learning "Simple Gifts" is that the notes don't jump around a lot. Even though there are many notes, this makes it easier. Because of the many notes you may think this song moves fast. It doesn't. Think moderate tempo.

In 1963, Sydney Carter wrote lyrics to the melody of "Simple Gifts." His "Lord of the Dance" generally has a faster tempo and a dance-like feeling.

Long, Long Ago
Most Popular Song in America in 1843

Tune D A A

Thomas Haynes Bayly (1797-1839)

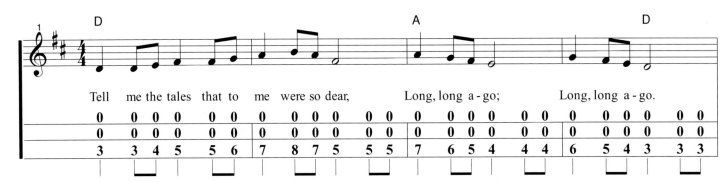

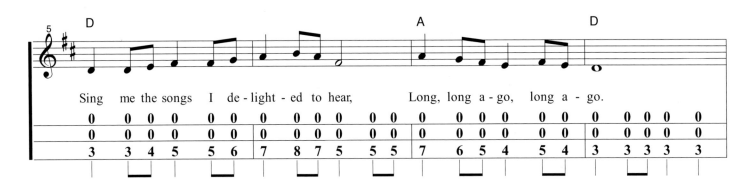

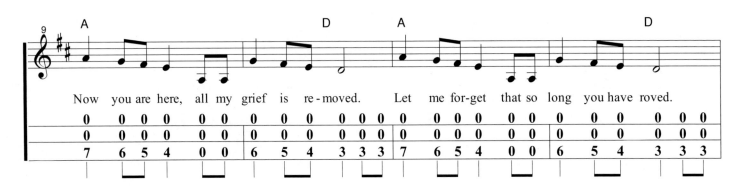

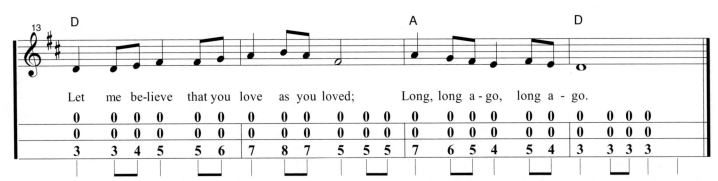

Do you remember the paths where we met?
Long, long ago; long, long ago.
Ah, yes, you told me you'd never forget,
Long, long ago, long ago.
Then to all others, my smile you preferred.
Love, when you spoke, gave a charm to each word.
Still my heart treasures the phrases I heard,
Long, long ago, long ago.

Tho' by your kindness my fond hopes were raised,
Long, long ago; long, long ago.
You by more eloquent lips have been praised,
Long, long ago, long ago.
But, by long absence your truth has been tried.
Still to your accents I listen with pride.
Blessed as I was when I sat by your side,
Long, long ago, long ago.

Red River Valley

Carl Sandberg: "I have heard it sung as if bells might be calling across a mist in the gloaming."

Tune D A A

Traditional American Song

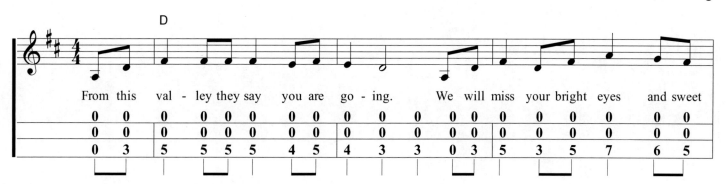

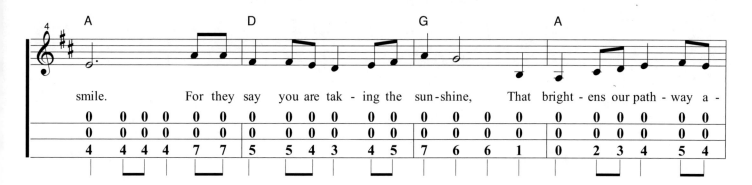

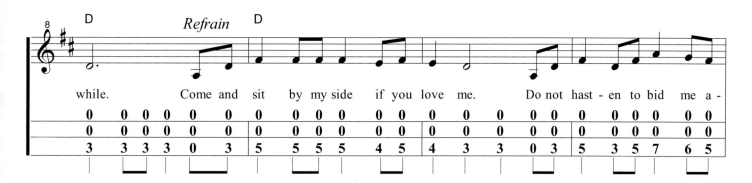

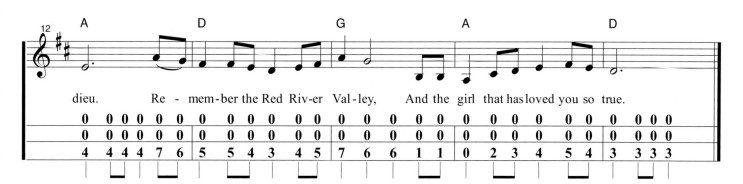

Do you think of the valley you're leaving?
Oh, how lonely, how sad it will be.
Oh, think of the fond heart you're breaking,
And the grief you are causing to me.
Refrain:

As you go to your home by the ocean,
May you never forget those sweet hours
That we spent in the Red River Valley,
And the love we exchanged 'mid the flowers.
Refrain:

19

Be Thou My Vision

Tune D A A

Traditional Irish

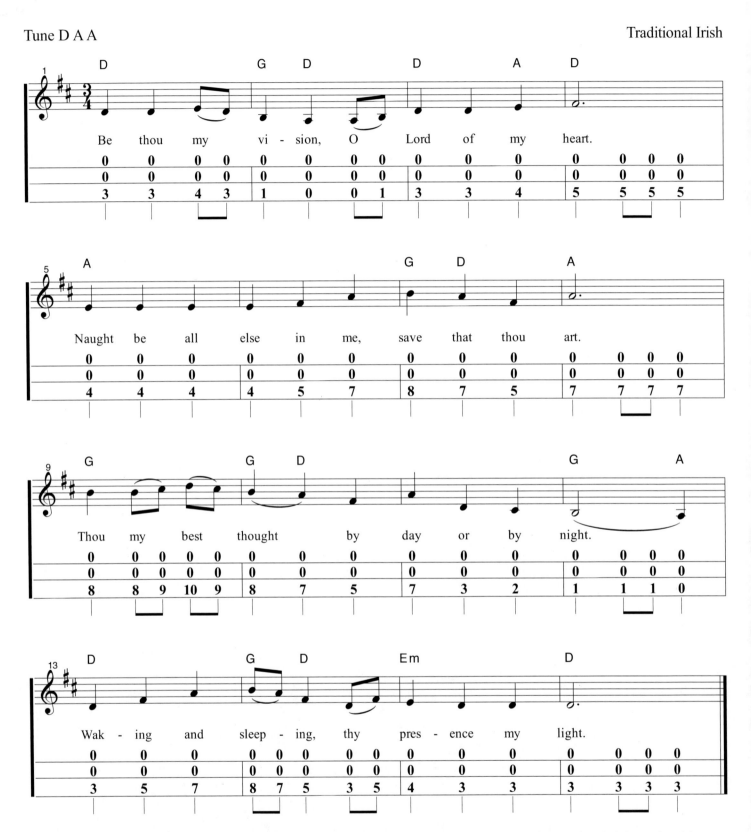

This beautiful song has quite a history accompanying it. The original Irish text may have been part of the Irish monastic tradition before it became an actual hymn. The most common English text used today for the song was adapted in 1912. The tune was originally called "Slane," after a hill in Ireland.

You are using a wide range of the dulcimer for this song, taking you from the open melody string to the 10th fret. This is a time to re-evaluate your holding of the instrument so the higher frets will be easier to play. Refer to the section in the front of the book about holding the dulcimer comfortably on your lap.

Waterbound

Before playing this song, read the paragraph at the bottom

Tune D A A   Traditional Appalachian Song

Play this song A A B

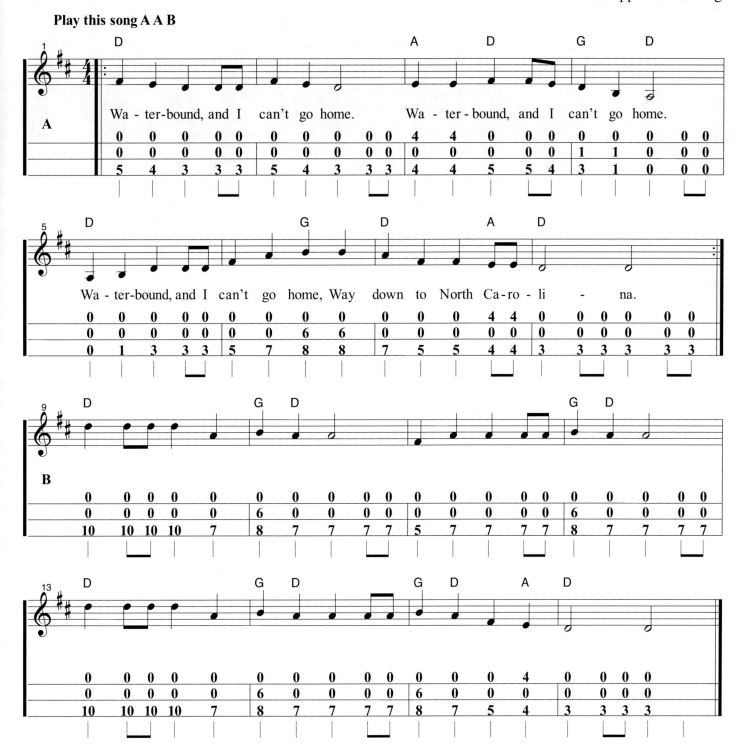

There are several learning opportunities with this song. First, I want you to refer to the arrangement for "Old Joe Clark" in this book (page 26). We discuss repeats and how they are indicated. This song has a repeat, and "Waterbound and I can't go home..." is the refrain. Here's how to play the song: Play the first 8 meansures (the A part) with no words. Then repeat it and sing "Waterbound...." Then play the B part (the last two lines). When you're singing the verses below, sing the verse, then sing "Waterbound...," then play the B part!

The song also has some chords for you to try. This well-loved song for dulcimer players was the first one I learned to play.

A • Chickens a-crowing in the old plowed field. (3x)
   Way down to North Carolina.
A • Waterbound...
B • *Play measures 9-16*

A • Water's up and I can't get across. (3x)
   Way down to North Carolina.
A • Waterbound...
B • *Play measures 9-16*

Changing Strings

This isn't an easy adventure, but after some tries you'll feel more confident. There is something I want you to do first: measure the vibrating string length of your dulcimer. This is important information not only for the purchasing of strings, but for helping you make decisions if you purchase another dulcimer. What does that mean? Perhaps a shorter fretboard is easier for you, especially when playing chords, if your fingers are short.

The vibrating string length is the part of the string where you can play music—between the Nut and the Bridge.

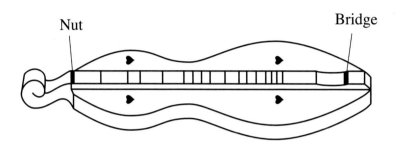

I assume the vibrating string length of your dulcimer is somewhere between 25 and 29 inches.

Now look at the right end of your dulcimer, where the strings attach to the instrument. The strings most often have loops at the end that fit over tiny nails. Every now and then instead of the loop end there's a ball end, which is important to know when you're buying strings.

Look at the bass string and run a fingernail up and down a portion of it. You'll most likely hear a "squeak." This means the string is a wound string. Do the same with the middle or melody string and you won't hear the squeak. These strings aren't wound.

You can purchase strings in sets from dulcimer shops in person or online. Be sure to look at the specifications on the envelope. Does the vibrating string length of your dulcimer come close to what they say? For example, if your dulcimer vibrating string length is 29 inches and the package says something like, "For up to a 28-inch scale," those aren't the strings for you. You're possibly better off buying the strings individually at a music store in your area. (More about that later.)

Let's proceed to the string sizes, beginning with the bass string. The general string sizes for dulcimers are .022W, .024W and .026W. (The W stands for Wound.) If you have a short-to-moderate vibrating string length dulcimer, .024W is good for starters. For very long dulcimers, try .022W for the bass string.

For the middle string (again, remember the vibrating string length of your dulcimer), .014 or .013 are good.

For the melody string, more considerations come into mind. We'll soon explore the DAD dulcimer tuning, which means the melody string(s) will be tuned to higher pitches. If you're staying in DAA, .013 or even the .014 are good options. If you wish to play often in DAD, .012 or, for a longer dulcimer, .011 are good choices.

If you go to a music store, here is what you say for most dulcimers after greeting the nice person who will help you. "I wish to purchase some loop-end strings. I want one .024 wound; one .014 and two .012." If you find, later on, that you'd like to try "larger" or "smaller" strings, follow your instinct.

Again, you'll need help the first time or more that you change strings. Don't be afraid to ask. How often do you change strings? This depends on how often you play the instrument. Let's toss out "every six months" for a starter. You want to keep the sound fresh. Always have back-up strings in case you break one.

DAD Tuning

We've mentioned before that most players in today's dulcimer world play tunes and songs in DAD rather than DAA tuning. They're both wonderful tunings, and the decision is yours in the long run. I've been a player who loves both tunings, so here's what I've done. I have four equidistant strings on my dulcimer and in essence have tuned the strings so I have both DAA and DAD.

	1	2	3	4	5
Bass String — D					
Middle String — A					
Middle String — A					
Melody String — D					

Maddie's Dulcimer
Bass String: D below Middle C
Both Middle Strings: A below Middle C
Melody String: D just above Middle C

In DAD tuning, the first two strings (the bass and the middle) are the same pitches as for the DAA tuning. The melody string is changing its pitch to the D just above Middle C.

Here they are:
D • below Middle C
A • below Middle C
D • just above Middle C

We'll explore the differences in these tunings (DAA and DAD), but the *primary* difference is that you'll now be using the 6+ fret for *Ti* in the *Do Re Mi…* scale. What if you don't have a 6+ fret but want to play tunes in DAD? That Ti note (C# in the musical scale) can be found on your middle string at the 9th fret. This takes a little hopping about, but it works.

I've heard some dulcimer players state opinions about these two tunings, DAA and DAD. I stick up for them both, for they both have advantages and disadvantages.

The DAA tuning has a rich texture because of the doubled 5th tone of the D scale. That's the A. You also have several notes below *Do* available on the melody string. Think of the song "Amazing Grace." The frets for the first notes, "Amazing grace, how sweet the sound," on the melody string are: 0 3 5 3 5 4 3 1 0. In DAD, you move to the middle string for some of the notes.

But DAD has its advantages also. When a tune is fairly "jumpy," meaning it moves a lot up and down, you can work with notes on the middle string. This keeps you from running up and down the fretboard so much.

Let's do some comparisons. Think *Do Re Me Fa Sol La Ti Do*. Musically these notes on our dulcimers are in the key of D: D E F# G A B C# D

In DAA tuning on the melody string you play D E F# G A B C# D via these frets: 3 4 5 6 7 8 9 10

In DAD tuning on the melody string you play D E F# G A B C# D via these frets: 0 1 2 3 4 5 6+ 7

Remember when we discussed tuning in the early part of this book? Go back and read that section again (remembering the word "gently") before tuning to DAD!

Down In The Valley
Comparison of DAA and DAD Tunings

Traditional

Down In The Valley • DAA tuning

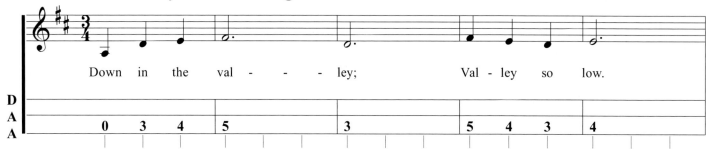

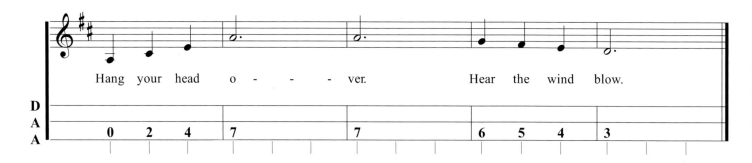

Down In The Valley • DAD tuning

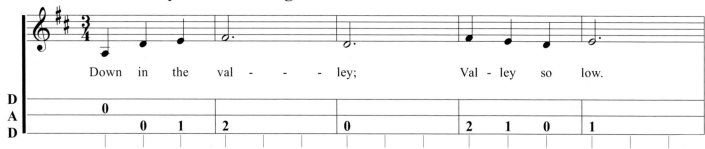

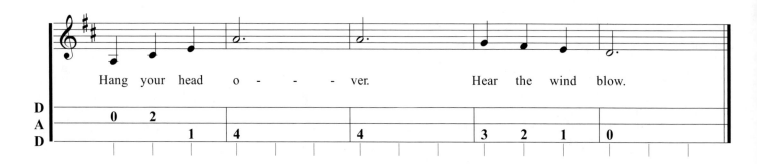

I've written out a basic tablature for this song so you can see how the left-hand fingers are in different places on the dulcimer fretboard to play the melody. In **DAA**, *Do* (as in *Do Re Mi...*) begins at the 3rd fret on the melody string. In **DAD**, *Do* begins on the open melody string. Therefore, notes lower than *Do* have to be played on the middle string, or possibly on the bass string if it's a very low note.

If you've tuned to **DAD**, you can still try this song as written above for **DAA** without retuning. In **DAD**, the middle string is tuned to A—just like your middle and melody strings in **DAA**, so you can play the **DAA** notes on your middle string. If I've lost you here, just give it a try! I want to hear you say, "Oh...," even if you say it quietly.

Boil That Cabbage Down
Dulcimer Players's National Anthem, in DAA and DAD

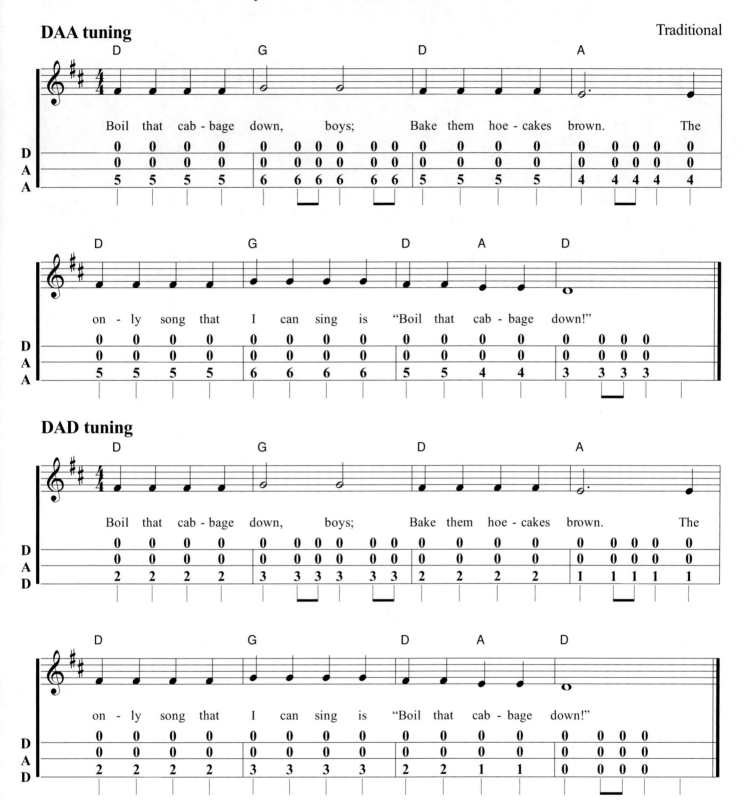

A "hoecake" is a coarse cake made of cornmeal. It was originally baked on the blade of a hoe.

I've never met a dulcimer player who didn't know this song. It's the one most of us learn first. I put it in the DAD section of the book because I want you to be able to play it in either DAA *or* DAD!

Old Joe Clark

This is a Favorite DAD Tune Enjoyed by Dulcimer Players
Take Note of Repeat Signs and How They Are Indicated

Tune D A D

Traditional

Play A A B B

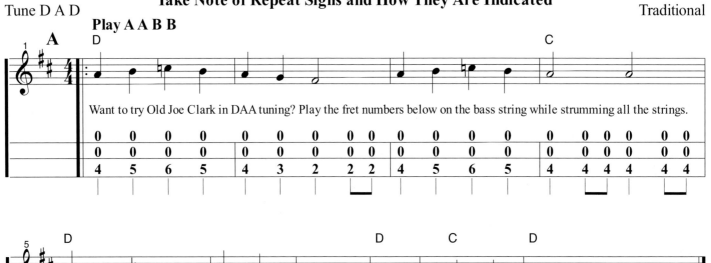

Want to try Old Joe Clark in DAA tuning? Play the fret numbers below on the bass string while strumming all the strings.

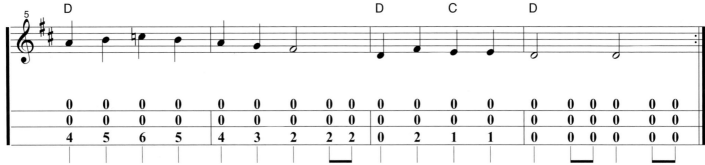

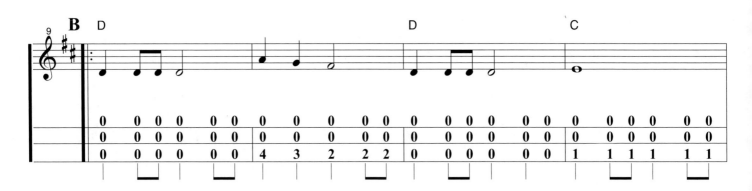

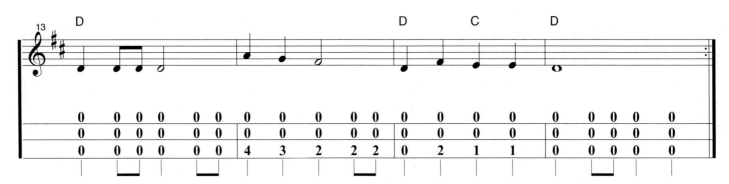

"Old Joe Clark" is repeated when you play it, and I've indicated it in two ways. You'll most likely see one way or the other in tunes that are repeated. First, look at the end of the 8th measure (measure numbers are at the beginning of each line). There is a double line with two dots on the left. This means you go back to a double line with two dots on the right, which you'll find that at the beginning. Repeat measures 1-8, then continue. At the end of measure 16 you see the same double line with dots, so you go back to measure 9 and repeat measures 9-16.

I've also "named" these areas A and B. At the top you see "Play A A B B." This means you play the A section twice and the B section twice. You've done the same as you did with the repeat lines/dots.

26

Brahms' Lullaby

Tune D A D _____ *This is generally the place where we're told which tuning to use.* Johannes Brahms (1833-1897)

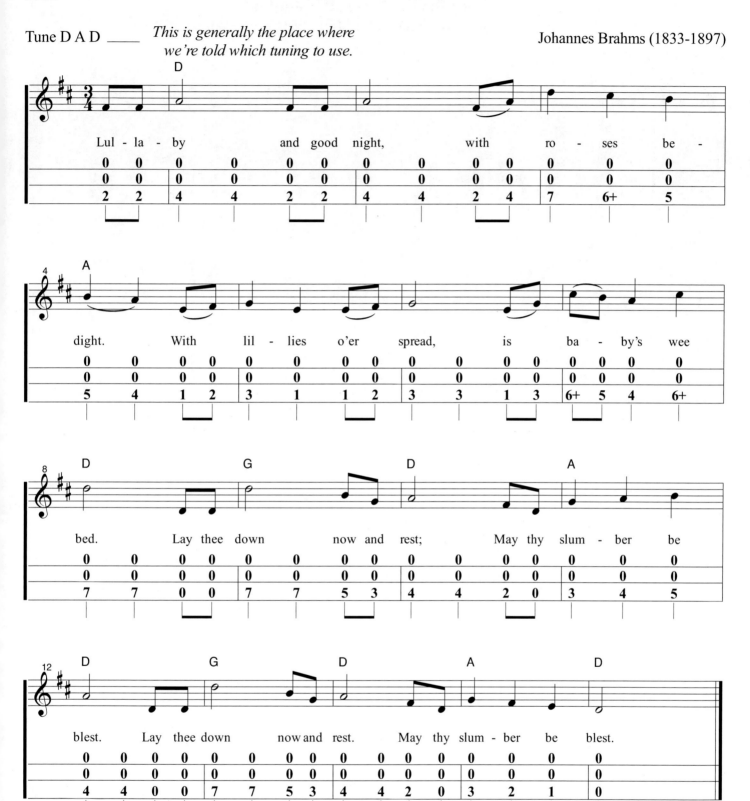

I used the DAD tuning for this beautiful song especially because of the large jumps between frets. You'll be using the 6+ fret a few times, so this is an opportunity to get more familiar with its location. This song doesn't go below the open melody string, so if you're more comfortable with DAA tuning, play the melody notes on the bass string and strum all of the strings.

Mississippi Sawyer

Another Tune with Repeated Sections
Melody Note Moves to the Middle String, Measures 11 and 12

Tune D A D

Play A A B B

Fiddle Tune

Remember when I told you that we all tend to do the strumming of tunes how it fits us right? You could say the same about this fiddle tune. If you hear six individuals play "Mississippi Sawyer" as a solo, you'll hear, probably, six variations—especially if a fiddle player is tossed into the mix. I don't remember the tune or the place, but one time I heard somebody tell us we were playing the tune "incorrectly." That's not how it was played in his or her hometown! The basic tune is close to what is played wherever, but we all have to learn to adapt sometimes. This makes folk music special, for we *all* make it our own.

Where to Go From Here

Problem

You're at a jam session tuned DAD and you're given some dulcimer tablature in DAA. Perhaps re-tuning isn't the easiest option for you right now, or perhaps you feel more comfortable playing in DAD, but you want to play the melody you've been given.

Solution

Your middle string is tuned to A, and those folks playing the tune are playing it on a string tuned to A. It just happens to be the melody string for them. So you play the tune on your string which is tuned to A. That's the middle string in DAD tuning. Not only does this work, but you add some nuance to the overall sound. You possibly can't include the chords, but the melody is easily there.

Problem

You're at a jam session tuned DAA and you're given some dulcimer tablature in DAD. Perhaps re-tuning isn't the easiest option for you right now, or perhaps you feel more comfortable playing in DAA. But you want to play the melody you've been given.

Solution

Your bass string is tuned to D, and the folks playing the tune are using their melody string which is tuned to D. You can play most of the melody on your bass string, the D string. There's a little catch here. Remember when we tuned to DAD from DAA and some melody notes went to the middle string? You're going to run out of notes when you get to the open bass string. But this won't happen too often. Just wait until the notes return to where you can play them on the bass string.

On pages 30 and 31 of this book there are two arrangements of "Twinkle, Twinkle Little Star." One is in DAA tuning while the other is in DAD. The tunings will be well-marked here, but this is a reminder to check the top left (it's generally there) of dulcimer music to determine the needed tuning for an arrangement. There will be chords in each arrangement, in case you'd like to include them in your playing.

Play either the DAA or DAD arrangement, or try playing the melodies on the middle or bass string as we discussed above.

On the CD several of us will play "Twinkle, Twinkle Little Star" three times. (We call that *three passes*.) Near the end of the last pass, you'll hear, "We're going home." That means we're approaching the end of the song. You are performing with us, so after we strum the last note hold your pick in the air and smile. All of us will be appreciated.

Twinkle, Twinkle Little Star
DAA Tuning with Optional Chords

Tune D A A

English Lullaby

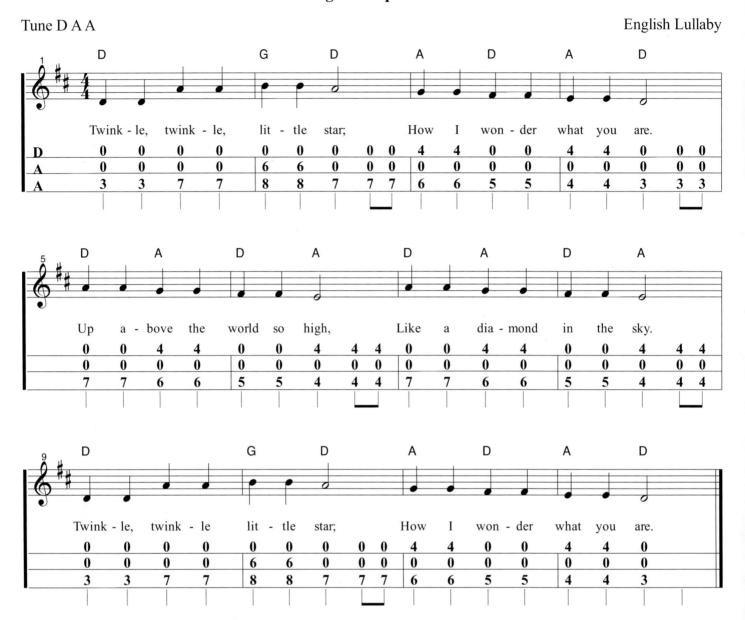

The lyrics for "Twinkle, Twinkle Little Star" were written in England by Jane Taylor in 1806. It is sung to the tune of a French melody which was later arranged by Wolfgang Amadeus Mozart into a set of variations.

As I mentioned before, several of us will be playing "Twinkle, Twinkle Little Star" on the book's CD. We'll be playing in DAA and DAD, with and without the chords—all together. In part, this is to show you how the two tunings work well together and can enrich the music.

You choose the tuning you prefer, with or without the chords, and play along with us. We'll sound wonderful!

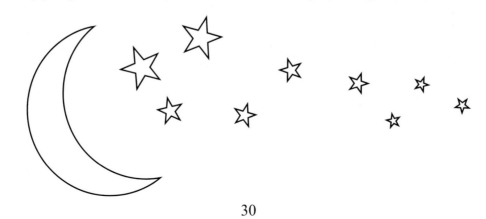

Twinkle, Twinkle Little Star
DAD Tuning with Optional Chords

Tune D A D

English Lullaby

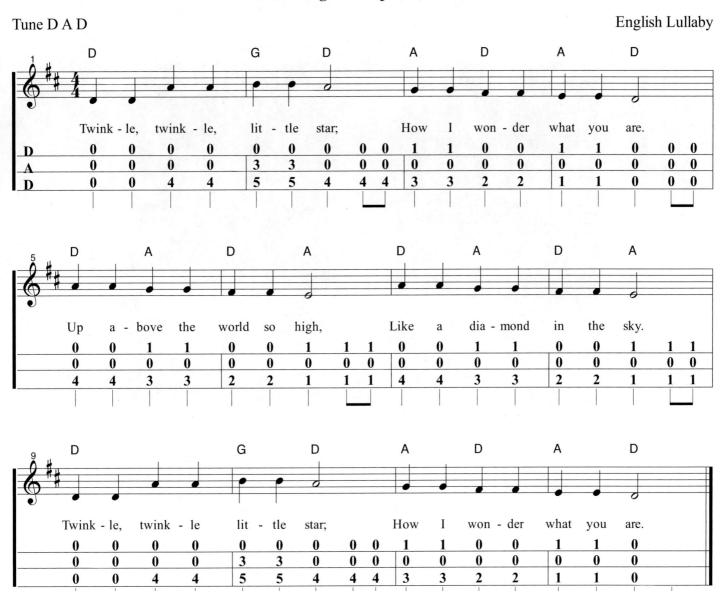

Here is something to remember when you're learning songs and tunes to play on the dulcimer. Explore the music, if possible. Knowing something about what we're playing actually helps us in more ways than one. Remember when we discussed the tempo for "Simple Gifts?" It appeared to be fast because of all of the notes. Reading the lyrics to "Simple Gifts," such as "When true simplicity is gained...," might give you ideas, as can a little research into the lives of the Shakers.

All of these findings and feelings about tunes and songs guide us. As we approach the end of this book, I encourage you to explore and to put what you find into your music.

There is a reason for all of us to share music with each other. Share your music with those young and old and in between. You'll be helping many of us. Thank you for coming along with me during this dulcimer journey. Play me a tune!

About the Author

Madeline MacNeil's own dulcimer journey began more than thirty years ago. Actually, the adventures first began when, in her mid-twenties, she decided that life as a folksinger would be more exciting than her profession as a high school educator! Maddie's guitar and her collection of LPs by Judy Collins, Joan Baez, Joni Mitchell and Peter, Paul and Mary accompanied her on the road—as far away as Virginia's Shenandoah National Park (40 miles). For six years she performed at Skyland Lodge in the Park. Then she began traveling to arts centers and festivals throughout the United States, making recordings, and writing books for Mel Bay Publications.

madelinemacneil.com